POETRY PICNIC

Vol. 2

Hayley Bartlett

ISBN-13: 9798440448087

Cover design by: Art Painter
Library of Congress Control Number: 2018675309
Printed in the United States of America

This book is dedicated to my late mother and to my late son
Gone but never forgotten!

CONTENTS

Title Page

Copyright

Dedication

Authors 4

Music 5

Heroes 6

Dreams 7

Tea 8

Poetry 9

Time 10

Ghosts 11

Caged 12

Slumber 13

Life 14

Milestones 15

Babies 16

Memory of Mother 17

Friendship 18

Family 19

Ode to Hermit Crabs 20

Horses 21

Doves   22

Turtles   23

Spiders   24

Summer   25

Rivers   26

H2O   27

Flowers   28

Trees   29

Stinky   30

Farts   31

Gas   32

Poop Matters   33

Feet   34

Marines   37

America   42

Freedom   44

Made in America   45

City of Dreams   46

Angels   47

Light of God   48

I Walk with You   50

Lamb of God/Agnus Dei   51

Our Lady, Mother most Holy   52

Blessings   53

A Writer's Prayer   54

The Visitor   55

Heaven   59

Take a Stand   60

Ukraine	61
Egypt	62
Luck O' the Irish	63
Germany	64
Australia	65
9 Planets	66
Space	67
Valentine's Day	68
About The Author	70
Books By This Author	72

Poetry Picnic Vol. 2

Miscellaneous Poems
- -Authors
- -Music
- -Heroes
- -Dreams
- -Tea
- -Poetry
- -Time
- -Ghosts

Serious Poems
- -Caged
- -Slumber
- -Life
- -Milestones
- -Babies
- -Memory of Mother
- -Friendship
- -Family

Nature Poems
- -Ode to Hermit Crabs
- -Horses
- -Doves
- -Turtles
- -Spiders
- -Summer
- -Rivers
- -H2O
- -Flowers
- -Trees

Silly Poems
- -Stinky
- -Farts
- -Gas

-Poop Matters
-Feet

Patriotic Poems
-The Presidents Pt. 1
-Marines
-The Presidents Pt. 2
-North vs South
-The Presidents Pt. 3
-America
-Freedom
-Made in America

Religious Poems
-City of Dreams
-Angels
-Light of God
-I Walk with You
-Lamb of God
-Our Lady, Mother Most Holy
-Blessings
-A Writer's Prayer
-The Visitor
-Catholic Children's Jokes Pt. 1
-Catholic Children's Jokes Pt. 2
-Heaven

Around the World/Political Poems
-Take a Stand
-Ukraine
-Egypt
-Luck O' the Irish
-Germany
-Australia

Space Poems
-9 Planets

HAYLEY BARTLETT

   -Space

Seasonal Poems
   -Valentine's Day
   -St. Patrick's Day

AUTHORS

Authors take readers to faraway lands
Near and far they take their audiences

To a fantasy world where nothing is as it seems
To outer space on a faraway planet

To a kingdom far, far away
Where the knights go on chivalrous adventures for maidens fair

Or maybe learn a new language, history of a far-off nation
Grab a classic about a black horse, or a fawn

Maybe some poetry
Or solve a mystery

Wonderful authors like John Steinbeck, Emily Bronte, Charles Dickens, and many others
Poets of world renown as Edgar Allen Poe and Longfellow

Grab a book, settle down
Find a comfortable chair

Take an adventure
Or learn something new

MUSIC

Music, the heart and soul the world over
One of the universal languages
Soothes the heart
Eases the pain

Music, sweet and melodic
Hypnotizes the listener
Stops the anger
Brings on peace

Music soft and dreamy
Brings on the sleep
With dreams so sweet
In solid slumber you will be

Music, time and tempo
To the beat people dance
Gather together to listen and enjoy
Brings the earth peace and joy

HEROES

Heroes come in all shapes and sizes
Real life heroes do not have superpowers
Real life heroes have normal everyday jobs
And they use their jobs to help us in need

Police Officers help keep order
They keep crime off the streets
Help crime victims
Keep people safe

Doctors help their patients get better
They ease discomfort and pain
Give you medicine when needed
And help keep you comfortable as you pass into the next world

Nurses help doctors with their duties
They will sit if you ask if they have time
The administer the medicine in hospitals
And they help ease anxiety

Firefighters try to help you out of a burning building
They put fires out with hoses and blasts of water
Get a cat out of a tree
And keep doing it without fear

Paramedics get you to the hospital in an emergency
They treat you on the scene if needed
Administer the medicines they are trained to do
They do it all with quickness and care

DREAMS

Dreams can be nice and entertaining

They can also be bad and terrifying

Dreams can lead to a lifetime achievement

Or a goal to be accomplished

Dreams can be messages from God, or a deceased loved one

They can also be menacing traps from demons or nothing at all

Sometimes dreams can be the key to unlocking our mental health

How we feel in our lives… happy and satisfied

Unhappy and discouraged

The constant dance of the Id and the Ego

One speaks in the day, and the other at night

But worry not, the meanings are not as complicated as they appear

TEA

Tea is very great for the body

It is very healing and relaxing

Herbal teas are especially good

Helps the body fight many ailments

Protects against others

Relieves stress and anxiety

Though tea is an acquired taste, it is very beneficial

Medicine without side effects

The best kind of all

POETRY

Many different authors have written poetry

With many different tones

Dark tones

Light tones

And even in between

Poetry is the window into the poets thoughts

How they describe the world around them

Their feelings

How things affect them

But put in a very beautiful way

TIME

Time is endless

Man can manipulate time

Time passes

It can pass fast or slow

People age over time

The most important thing about time

Is that no matter what time keeps marching on

GHOSTS

Ghosts rule the night

They affect our dreams

Scare us

Make great campfire story topics

Make our imaginations run wild

Get the hair on the backs of our necks stand on end

Though there is no such thing as the ghosts of scary stories

The Holy Ghost is real and pleasant

CAGED

Trapped like an animal inside thoughts and emotions

To a relationship now scorned

Raw fury gives good people a bad action to do

The clock cannot be turned back to take it away

Fear is locked inside where happiness once dwelt

What is done is done

It cannot be undone

No amount of time can heal the fear

Untouchable does intimacy kill

Being forever broken is inevitable

No amount of love can fix what is broken

Too much patience and time is required

Time to say goodbye

The fun was truly fun and enjoyable

The experiences were new and exciting

But a line was crossed

And we are past the point of rescue

In the cage of fear, no one wants to dwell

SLUMBER

Slumber comes creeping softly
To dreamland so lofty

Slumbering to heights unknown
To what I have known

Slumber in the night
Though my dreams give me fright

Slumbering through the day
Trying to get away from the fray

Slumber to escape my thoughts
With danger in remembering

Slumber to escape the dark feeling
Consuming my very soul

Slumber to ease anxiety
Keeping my body calm

Slumber to runaway
To Die? Nay

Slumber, slumber to keep the bad thoughts at bay.

LIFE

Life, something that begins at the moment of conception

Growing for nine months in a temperature-controlled organ

Once born, life continues

Going from infancy to toddlerhood

In infancy, crawling; in toddlerhood learning to walk

With walking mastered, running becomes a pastime.

Now comes adolescence, and with it, puberty

The body makes changes be it boy or girl, but the changes are different

Those teenage years are beyond reproach, getting used to growth spurts and acne

Now, fully grown... time for a job, a spouse, and a family all your own

Parents have passed but life goes on

That's life! Go live it up while you can

MILESTONES

Milestones reached

Too many to count

Of the ones you are no longer here to witness

How I want to share them with you

Oh, how my heart aches, thinking about you

Being here to share in the happy times

But you are gone

Gone too soon for my heart

Graduation, you could not be there

Marriage, though a bad one in the end, you could not share

A child made of love, you could not attend its birth

Life achievements you would be proud

Foreshadows my happiness

Wish you were here

To share the happy moments

BABIES

Babies are blessing from Heaven above

Full of endless energy and boundless love

With plenty of smiles and laughter

Wiggling and giggling

And giving a feeling of warmth and joy

MEMORY OF MOTHER

Mother you were always there
Anytime I needed you
You were there

When I fell and scraped my knee
You were there with band-aids and love
With kisses and hugs

When I broke a bone
In pain
You got me the help I needed and gave me much comfort

The cold and flu did not matter
You were there with soup and medicine
Taking the best care of me

We made cookies together
Played games
Laughed and cried together

Gone you are
The memories of you I hold onto
The love and warmth you gave me I keep in my heart

I reach milestones and think of you
Wishing you were there by my side as you always were
Cheering me on and guiding me in my dreams and goals

FRIENDSHIP

Friends come in all different sizes

They are there for you when you need them

Guiding you and supporting you in your desires

When you achieve a goal, they are there to celebrate with you

Suffer a loss and they cry with you

Need some assistance and they help when and where they can

Friendships are the best things to have

FAMILY

Families are supposed to have your back

They should not turn away

And love unconditionally

But sometimes

Family turns their back on you when you need them most

When you are struggling from a loss

Instead, they blame you

When they should have been helping, they leave the work all to you

Like the Little Red Hen, if they are not going to do their share, they do not get to help reap the rewards

ODE TO HERMIT CRABS

Hermit crabs,
You make the best pets
The personality traits you possess are so interesting

No single hermit crab acting like the others
Nice and sweet
Very engaging with their humans

No sweeter love than a hermit crab that snuggles in your hands during exercise time
So curious about the world around you, yet cautious in your approach
Even sometimes being afraid of your own shadow

That is okay!
The smiles you put on my face
Seeing you play in your miniature habitat

Watching all of you interact is better than going to a circus
Keeping you healthy is my goal
And happy, I plan to keep you into your old age

As with any pet, I will never abandon you in your hour of need
To the very end, though as long as I have had you it will hurt to say goodbye

But, for all your life, I will be there
As you have for me since the moment, I brought you home

HORSES

Horses are majestic and strong

Bonded with their rider like no other

They can carry heavy loads

Or carry a rider on their back.

Horses can pull carts, wagons, and plows

They can tell when you are down and depressed

Horses also like to hang with other horses

Carrots and apples are treats for them and treats for us

A stone in their hoof can make them lame

As can throwing a shoe

Take care of your horse and your horse will take care of you

DOVES

Doves are very pretty birds

They have many different meanings

Doves are a symbol of peace

Sometimes they are used in wedding ceremonies

They are mostly pure white

And they can bond with people

Noah used a dove to see if the water had gone down after the rain had been done for a while

It returned with an olive branch

TURTLES

Turtles are very amazing creatures

They can breathe through their rears

Dive under water

Hold their breath for a decent amount of time

They can make good pets for the experienced turtle person

There are many different species

Painted turtles are the best aquatic turtles to keep

Depending on the species they can get very big, but start off life so tiny

SPIDERS

Spiders are little creatures with eight legs

They can cause some people nightmares

But they serve a purpose

They keep the bug population down

Without spiders humans would be overrun by all kinds of bugs

The great majority of spiders are harmless to humans other than a painful bite

Some are dangerous to humans, but not that many

If you have a bug infestation problem

And you want to avoid using chemical filled bug spray, maybe adopt a spider or two into your house

They'll eat the bugs and enjoy the constant room temperature and in return for rent, they eat the pests

SUMMER

Summer is for time in the sun

Pool parties are for friends to have fun

When people are out smelling the flowers

And lovers are out taking walks

The bees are buzzing

Dogs are barking in the park

Birds are having little cheeps

Children ride their bikes

Waiting for the ice cream man to bring the treats

In the nighttime the fireflies come out

And everyone enjoys trying to catch them

Then its off to bed to get some rest

To get some energy for the days ahead

RIVERS

Rivers flow to places of adventure

Nile river so long bringing fertile soil to Egypt in a flood

Amazon river with its flora and fauna so abundant and beautiful

Boats can take be taken for wild river adventures

White water rafting anyone?

Traveling to another part of the country, maybe sail down a river

The peaceful tranquility

The endless destinations to choose from

The quiet

Open for meditation as you travel

Full of dinner if when hungry

Sleep on the bank when tired

Rivers full of water, adventure, and peace

H2O

Water the foundation of life

It satisfies thirst

Helps flowers to grow

Falls from the sky in a storm

Comes in many a different form

Liquid water, vapor, snow, and ice

Animals and humans alike need water to stay hydrated

The human body is made up of about eighty percent water

The scientific term for water is H2O because it takes two hydrogen atoms and one oxygen atom

Thank the Lord for water

FLOWERS

Flowers come in all shapes and sizes

They come in all different hues

Petunias have a wide variety of colors

Sunflowers only come in different shades of yellow

Tulips come in a rainbow explosion

Daffodils are mostly yellow with some varieties being orange and cream

Collecting flowers to make a bouquet is okay

Just make sure to ask before you pick them

TREES

Trees, trees everywhere

All around the world, trees

A forest is not a forest without its trees

Rainforests suffer with deforestation, loss of trees

Even beaches have their palm trees

Oases also have their trees

Pine trees, fruit trees, maple trees, oak trees

Trees, trees everywhere

STINKY

Poop is stinky
Skunks are stinky
But we live with it

Stinkbugs smell
As does skunkweed
But we live with it

Some poop is smellier than others
Some just pass that gag reflex from the olfactory organ
But we live with it

Skunks do not want to smell themselves
Neither do we want to smell our poop
But we live with it

Babies poop stinks horrible
As do our pets
But we live with it

Politicians can have stinky ideas
As can world leaders
But we live with it

War stinks
Crime stinks
But we live with it

But just because we live with it
Does not mean we have to like it

FARTS

Root toot-toot!
Here come the farts

Over and yonder!
Here come the farts

Always coming, never ceasing!
Here come the farts

Rumbling in the tummy gotta let it go!
Here come the farts

Pressure after every meal need relief!
Here come the farts

Stinky as they go losing friends with every single one!
Here come the farts

There they go, think I'm done!
There go the farts

GAS

Natural gas powers cars

Diesel powers most trains and trucks

Buses and some cars

But there is a type of gas that our bodies let off

It is a part of natural digestion

Sometimes our bodies pass it naturally

Other times our bodies need a little help

Some cultures find burping and farting after a meal a sign of politeness

It signifies that the meal was very good

They find it rude if you don't

So, remember when travelling to another country and you are a guest in someone's home

You do not always have to try to hold it in

POOP MATTERS

Everyone is joining the Black lives matter movement
A racist movement.
All lives should matter
The majority of us have families

So, What about poop.
Everyone poops
Every animal poops
It helps take toxic waste out of the body

Waste needs to be excreted no matter what color our skin is
So, I say poop matters
Poop is the only thing that should matter
It keeps all our bodies healthy when it exits the body

Healthy poop is the same healthy brown color
No matter what color human it comes out of
Poop brown is poop brown
So, from the word of the poop turd, Poop, poop, poopity-doop

FEET

Big feet

Small feet

Clean feet

Smelly feet

Wide feet

Slim feet

Athlete's foot

Twelve inches in a foot

Now you have the facts on feet

The Presidents Pt. 1

George Washington, the first president and the most liked by his constituents

John Adams, second president of the United States, first president to call the White House home

Thomas Jefferson, third president and author of the Declaration of Independence

James Madison, fourth president, co-author of The Federalist Papers

James Monroe, fifth president and final founding father to hold the executive office

John Quincy Adams, sixth president and son of John Adams, lawyer and career politician in the good sense

Andrew Jackson, seventh president, with a temper unlike any other in defense of women's honor

Martin van Buren, eighth president very humble and wise took everything he did in stride

William Henry Harrison, ninth president oldest president in his day, and the first to die in office holds the record for shortest term

John Tyler, president number ten by default as being vice president to a long winded, common sense lacking president

James K. Polk, eleventh president last strong president to serve in peace time between the war of 1812 and the Civil War

Zachary Taylor twelfth president and a hero of two wars became the second president to die in office

Millard Filmore number thirteen so unlucky second vice president to succeed a sitting president due to death

Franklin Pierce fourteenth president hoped to hold off the impending Civil War which worked until the 1860s

James Buchanan fifteenth president the one and only from Pennsylvania and never married

Abraham Lincoln had a tough presidency as number sixteen a president during the major portion of the Civil War and Great Emancipator

Andrew Johnson took over after the Lincoln assassination as the seventeenth president and never had a Vice President

Ulysses S. Grant war hero of the North and eighteenth president of the United States.

MARINES

Marines strong and true
Answering the call of the red, white, and blue
Sacrificing their lives
Left behind are their wives

Marines sure and pure
For their country, in pain they quietly endure
Unending bravery
To end all things including slavery

Marines past and present
United by the uniform many nations resent
Love and honor
Sister and brother

Marines fought the good fight
Now the day turns to night
As you slip to the Heavens
Angels escort you in warm successions

Marines in Heaven we love, cherish and miss you
In the end a better place embraces the navy blue
Done with war
In a new corps.

Goodnight, Marines
We say goodbye to the fallen
As tears roll down the cheeks
Nothing but sorrow fills the coming weeks

The Presidents Pt. 2

Rutherford B. Hayes nineteenth president worked on rebuilding the South and retired after only serving one term

James A. Garfield twentieth president one of many from Ohio and was assassinated while in office

Chester A. Arthur twenty-first president of the United States who took over after the death of Garfield and did not have a Vice President serving with him

Grover Cleveland twenty-second president had a vice president for only a small portion of his term

Benjamin Harrison twenty-third president grandson of William Henry Harrison

Grover Cleveland once again became president to be number twenty-four

William McKinley president twenty-five another Ohioan who was another president to die in office from an assassin's bullet

Theodore (Teddy) Roosevelt was the twenty-sixth president and for part of his term he had no vice president because he had taken over for McKinley

William Howard Taft twenty-seventh president sometimes rumored to have been stuck in a white house bathtub at one point

Woodrow Wilson number twenty-eight leader during World War I

Warren G. Harding president twenty-nine and the first president to be caught up in a scandal during his term and died in office

Calvin Coolidge was the thirtieth president when he took over for Harding and was in office at the start of the Great Depression when the stock market started to tank in 1929

Herbert Hoover served as the thirty-first president and great humanitarian

Franklin Delano Roosevelt number thirty-two served a groundbreaking four terms in office despite being wheelchair bound due to having survived polio

Harry S. Truman president thirty-three took us through the war in Korea

Dwight D. Eisenhower was the thirty-fourth president helped bring about a truce in Korea and tried to forge a semi friendship with Russia during the cold war

John F. Kennedy thirty-fifth president was well-liked, though he faced great odds being an Irish Catholic

North vs. South

During the time of the Civil War

America was split into two parts

The United States of America

And the Confederate states

Between 1861 and 1863 many Americans on both sides lost their lives

Still called the bloodiest war in American history

Caused Abraham Lincoln to lose his life needlessly

Eventually the two halves of the whole came back together

But to this day some disgust still remains

The Presidents Pt. 3

Lyndon B. Johnson president number thirty-six had a little jingle associated with him do to the issues during the Vietnam war

Richard Nixon thirty-seventh president known most for the Watergate scandal, was going to get impeached, but as a decent man, stepped down

Vice President Gerald Ford took over the rest of Nixon's term as president number thirty-eight

Jimmy Carter the peanut farmer became the thirty-ninth president and had previously served in the Navy

Ronald Reagan was president number forty he was an actor and former governor

Geroge H.W. Bush took the forty-first presidential spot with his famous words, "Read my lips, no new taxes,"

Bill Clinton dumbest president for not knowing certain things about certain things, but something great to make fun of... keep it in your pants Clinton was president number forty-two

Geroge W. Bush forty-third president with his heart in the right place of no child left behind in education made the public-school grading system a convoluted nightmare

Barack I never showed my proper birth certificate Obama was number forty-four, but that is very questionable

Donald Trump, forty-fifth president was good in some ways like trying to keep stimulus money in America… but bad in others

Joe Biden at number forty-six was vice president under Obama, has done little to nothing to combat COVID-19 and has not even tried to calm Putin and his greed

And that is all the presidents of the United States for now

AMERICA

America the land of golden opportunity
The land of heroes and dreams
Of bravery, honor, and freedom

America, the once great nation of people accepting history for what it was
No cover ups, makeovers, or rewrites
Where the great Martin Luther King, Jr. made a speech of racial equality for all
With his legacy being marred by black and white alike

With people who had slaves in a time when it was acceptable being called horrendous names
People who have moved past it from over a century and a half ago
Now once again dealing with it, though instead of whites being racist the other party is being equally shameful

America a place where everyone should have the same freedoms and rights who are straight and care about children both in the womb and out
A place where no matter the skin color, everyone should call each other brother and sister without angst and anger
A land that wants to rid itself of children bullying other children, but does not realize it needs to set the example for children to follow

As Americans we must stand united
End the violence
Teach the children to respect one another
Learn everyone's heritage to become truly

HAYLEY BARTLETT

One nation under God, completely indivisible with liberty and justice for all

43

FREEDOM

Freedom, our founding fathers wanted it

Colonists revolted for it

Patriots died for it

Soldiers fight for it

Government officials are supposed to uphold it

Freedom is never truly free

Freedom has a price, the price of sacrifice and life

George Washington and his compatriots would have been arrested for treason

Had they not won the fight

Ben Franklin and the allies he made in France gave us the extra power to turn the tide

So, Freedom could ring from sea to sea and down the mountainside

MADE IN AMERICA

Long ago, everything Americans used was made in their country

Jobs were abundant and people were happy

Christianity helped the country prosper

Churches were in charge of child placement

Abortions were unheard of

Homosexuals were beaten or imprisoned

They did not have any rights to begin with and should not have them now

Straight people do not have any special treatment so homosexual people should not either

Clothes, cars, gasoline, and many more products were made in America

Soldiers were stronger and proud to serve this great nation

The nation was much more prosperous

The economy was booming

Now things are made in China and other countries

Will anything be made in America again?

CITY OF DREAMS

In a field I lay
Watching the clouds roll by
Across the way is a city with lights
A city of hopes and aspirations
In the City of Dreams

How I wish I could get there
Bring my virtues and talents
Try my luck in acting
Or maybe a publisher for a book
In the City of Dreams

If I could, I would go
But here I lay in the field
Just dreaming of high hopes and dreams
Laying here thinking of all the things I could be
In the City of Dreams

As I lay here in this field
I grow very tired
Lounging in this field I take a nap
And see in my mind all the possibilities
In the City of Dreams

However, as I lay down and close my eyes
The City of Dreams starts to move
Closer, now closer still
Once I have drifted off now, I am
In the City of Dreams

ANGELS

Angels near me always
Angels near and far
Angels to watch over me
Angels to keep me strong

Angels walk with God
Angels talk to God
Angels praise God
Angels carry messages from God

Angels to guard us
Angels to pray for us
Angels to keep us in line
Angels to heal the weary souls

Angels always there for us
Angels to light the path
Angels to bring us peace
Angels to carry us home

LIGHT OF GOD

The light of God shines on the world
In peace and turmoil, the light of God smiles down

Down to all of His creation
He with them in their darkest hour

In riots and war people hide from the light of God
But it continues to shine

Through spring rains, sunny summer days, winter snow, and autumn leaves
The Light of God comes shining down

In His image he made all mankind; gave them paradise
But through greed humans destroyed it

With his love, He still continued to shine his light
And promised a Saviour to free them from sin

And through the suffering of Jesus Christ
God's light shone on humanity once more

With his love, he will heal us
With his mercy, he saves us
With his light, he guides us

Let God guide you with his light
Bring forth your love

Let him heal your sorrows
And bear your pain

Always remember that the light of God surrounds us in our daily

lives
And will not leave us in darkness unless we completely turn from
him

I WALK WITH YOU

Are you tired?

Are you burdened?

Are you worried?

I walk with you

Are you sad?

Are you afraid?

Are you persecuted?

I walk with you

Are you weary?

Are you lost?

Are you anxious?

I walk with you

From here to there, I walk with you

When you get so tired that you can no longer walk, I will carry you

LAMB OF GOD/ AGNUS DEI

Lamb of God take my sorrows

Lamb of God protect Ukraine

Lamb of God have mercy on us

Lamb of God shine your love upon us

Lamb of God grant us peace

Agnus Dei accipe dolores meos

Agnus Dei custodire Ucraina

Agnus Dei miserere nobis

Agnus Dei luceat lumen tuum super nos

Agnus Dei dona nobis Pacem

OUR LADY, MOTHER MOST HOLY

O Holy Mother,

Mother of the Son of God

Precious Gem

You cared so much for Jesus

A wonderful mother

Staying with him through it all

From very humble beginnings

To horrible crucifixion

How you must have wept

Seeing your Son upon that cross

Such unbearable pain in your heart

But from the time you presented him in the temple

You knew his fate

Strong you were and strong you are

O Mother of the Most High, Jesus Christ

BLESSINGS

Blessings raining down from Heaven

For all people here below

Blessings pouring into the soul

To share with the whole world

Blessings with each baby's first breath

To remind humanity of the miracle of life

Baby Jesus brought mankind many blessings

Fully grown He gave His life for all to open Heaven's Holy door

In the hopes that God's creation would all arrive there

But, alas, the very souls who are evil to the core

Do not gain any blessings, but burn all the more

A WRITER'S PRAYER

Dear God,

Help me this day to keep my writing on track

To please you using my talents that you gave me

No matter what genre I write, I should like it to please you

Guide my pen this day as I write and use my words to praise you

Thank you for giving me my talent

Thank you for giving me life

Thank you for your wonderful blessings

As I try to spread your words through the instruments I use

Amen.

THE VISITOR

I come to visit when you need me

You will never see me

But sometimes you may feel me

I visit you wherever you are

Even if you move, I know where you are

I am better than Santa Claus

I bring peace and love

I suffered, died, and rose again that from sin you might be free

I'm the silent visitor in the night

Always in your heart when invited in

When you are weary, come visit me

I will give you rest

Catholic Children's Jokes Pt. 1

I fought Satan and cast him out of Hell.
I have a whole prayer dedicated to me to ask for my help against evil
I have a higher rank than your guardian angel.
Who am I?

A: St. Michael the Archangel

I created the whole world in six days.
I made man in my own image.
I omnipresent, omnipotent, and omniscient
Who am I?

A: God

I have a whole day in my honor.
It is March 17th.
I am famously known for holding a shamrock in my hand.
Who am I?

A: Saint Patrick

God approached me through a burning bush.
I led the Israelites out of Egypt.
I received the ten commandments from God.
Who am I?

A: Moses

Catholic Children's Jokes Pt. 2

I was put into the Garden of Eden with Adam.
I was the first to eat the forbidden fruit.
I was made by God from one of Adam's ribs.
Who am I?

A: Eve

God changed my name and told me I'd be the father of all nations.
He changed my name and told me that in my old age my old wife
would have a child.
When my son was a young boy, God asked me to sacrifice him,
then God stopped me.
Who am I?

A: Abraham formerly known as Abram

We were enslaved in Egypt.
We were in the desert for what seemed like forever.
God rained down mana for us and gave us water to drink.
Who are we?

A: The Israelites

I was designed by God.
I held the ten commandments.
Only certain people could touch me.
What am I?

A: The Ark of the Covenant

HEAVEN

Heaven a home with God

With loved ones one and all

A happy place filled with God's great light

With angels singing all day long

Peace and Glad tidings all around

Unearthly joy one cannot fathom

It is too incredibly to truly understand

Until we go there, we can only dream

Of the beauties of Heaven that God and the angels see from day to day

TAKE A STAND

Take a stand for the flag of a nation
Take a stand for a cause
Take a stand against tyranny
Take a stand for Ukraine
Take a stand for the unborn children
Take a stand against human trafficking
Take a stand against dog fighting
Take a stand against inhumane slaughtering practices
Take a stand against Russia
Take a stand against Putin
Take a stand to end world hunger

Take a bow after a performance
Kneel for a prayer
Bow to a monarch

Take a stand end violence
Let's all take a stand with Ukraine

UKRAINE

Ukraine with you we stand
A nation born in the early nineties
Standing strong against a foe

With you we stand with our hearts and prayers
We stand with your men women and children
As you stand against the bear
Your pain we understand

From the USSR you were born
Over a decade tall you have stood
Tough as nails
Strong as your ancestors

Ukraine keep up your courage
Be an example for us all
How to stand against tyranny
How to be brave when all seems lost

A candle we hold for the people who lost their lives for Ukraine
Like the Polish did in World War II
Like the colonists did against the British
To stand together and show strength in perseverance.

EGYPT

Egypt so mysterious and grand
With Pharaohs and Pyramids
Sphynxes too!

A Desert and Oasis
Between Isis and Osiris
With camels and crocodiles

The river Nile so long and fertile
Brings the land great soil
The best soil in all the world

From Menes to Cleopatra
And all the leaders in between
Built Egypt up to its great glory

All the world in humble awe
Look to Egypt
To Learn about the lives of the ancient Egyptians

LUCK O' THE IRISH

Oh, the Irish, so majestic
With valleys of illustrious green hues
A beautiful coastline and folklore so amazing

With fairies, pixies, and leprechauns
Pots of gold and rainbows too
And lots of luck to go around.

Oh, the Irish with a grand flag of green, white and orange
A symbol of peace between Catholics and Protestants
A coming together of a country united

Oh, the Irish, so lucky to have a nation so beautiful
It's landscape a paradise in a non-tropical way
So simple, yet so elegant

To the Irish, may God always shine upon you
May the road rise up to greet you
And may the wind be ever at your back

GERMANY

Germany a home to many

Heroes fought and died

Hitler nearly destroyed you

Some of his men tried in vain to save you

Russia split Berlin in half

Ronald Reagan helped put it back together

Albert Einstein hailed from your beautiful nation

Famous in some part by the Swiss alps that help make your border

Wonderful countryside

Home to a great many things

Most famous for the Volkswagen

Most notably Herbie the Love Bug of Disney fame

AUSTRALIA

Australia, the land down under
Where the Crocodile Hunter hailed from
A place where kangaroos and wallabies hop

The Aboriginals play on their didgeridoos
And Ayres Rock sits majestic against the sunset
Where Koalas munch on eucalyptus leaves

Where poisonous snakes and spiders creep and crawl
And Crocodiles lie in wait for their prey
With a hospital to take care of sick and injured wildlife

Six climates makes up the continent
From tropical to temperate and in between
And very exquisite tourist attractions

Colorful birds, a variety of reptiles, unique mammals
Tasmanian Devils too!
All call Australia home.

9 PLANETS

Nine planets in the solar system

There is Mercury and Venus living in close proximity to the Sun

Then Earth is locked in the Goldilocks zone

People want to colonize Mars

And Jupiter has the big red spot

Saturn, Uranus, and Neptune all have rings around their equator

And Pluto has an identity crisis

SPACE

Space is a place full of sweet adventure

In a rocket ship, fly to the moon

Or to the International Space Station

Send a probe to Mars or any planet in between

Careful though, cause Jupiter, Uranus, Neptune, and Saturn are made of gas

Mercury and Venus are simply way to hot, the probe would melt

Stay away from the sun, it is the hottest thing in our space neighborhood

Pluto might be a good choice for a probe, but it is too cold for humans

Be wary of black holes, once they suck you in, they never let go

Asteroids have a deadly strike force

Comets are too fast no rocket could keep up

So next time, you look to the stars…

Imagine what adventures you may want to have

VALENTINE'S DAY

Red and pink hearts abound
Heart shaped boxes of chocolate
Love and romance is all around

Couples together
Going to dinner and movies
Or just cuddling at home with a romantic candlelight dinner

Cupid with his arrows
Looking to change singles to duos
Searching, searching he goes

Snow in most parts still lays on the ground
While in others it never was
Still Valentine's Day is celebrated

Love for one another
Children appreciate their parents
Grandparents too

Then the day is over
People go home
To wait for next year to show their love anew

HAYLEY BARTLETT

St. Patrick's Day

Saint Patrick's Day always falls on the seventeenth
Everyone wears green upon this glorious day
Catholics and non-Catholics alike dress in green out of tradition

All sorts of green decorations are put out
Leprechaun statues too
With rainbows and plastic pots o' gold

Some people go to church on this day to celebrate the man
Glorious Saint Patrick who went back to his former masters
Of whom he slaved away for until he managed to escape

Back to Ireland to teach the people about God
To convert them from their pagan ways
Promoted to Bishop, the Pope made him

With pure love, Saint Patrick was filled
Until his dying day
Preaching to the people with whom he was enamored

ABOUT THE AUTHOR

Hayley Bartlett

Hayley Bartlett loves writing so much, she just cannot stop. It started off as a hobby when she was a child. Now that hobby has grown.

That's great for people who like reading her work.

BOOKS BY THIS AUTHOR

Poetry Picnic Vol. 1

First book of the Poetry Picnic collection

All the poems in the first book were written in 2020 during the lockdown

Faith Morality: Ave Marie

Book 1 in the Faith Morality series for Catholic Children
Adults curious about Catholic prayers and rituals would find it enjoyable too.

Faith Morality: The Rosary

Book 2 in the Faith Morality series
Continues the teaching from book one with more adventures and lessons.